# ALL THINGS ANIME AND MANGA

# MANGA WORLD

**STUART A. KALLEN**

San Diego, CA

## About the Author

Stuart A. Kallen is the author of more than 350 nonfiction books for children and young adults. He has written on topics ranging from the theory of relativity to the art of electronic dance music. In addition, Kallen has written award-winning children's videos and television scripts. In his spare time he is a singer, songwriter, and guitarist in San Diego.

© 2024 ReferencePoint Press, Inc.
Printed in the United States

**For more information, contact:**
ReferencePoint Press, Inc.
PO Box 27779
San Diego, CA 92198
www.ReferencePointPress.com

ALL RIGHTS RESERVED.
No part of this work covered by the copyright hereon may be reproduced or used in any form or by any means—graphic, electronic, or mechanical, including photocopying, recording, taping, web distribution, or information storage retrieval systems—without the written permission of the publisher.

Picture Credits:
Cover: Rio Pamungkas

6: Lokyo Multimedia JP/Shutterstock
9: IanDagnall Computing/Alamy Stock Photo
12: NBC/Photofest
16: Cartoon Network/Photofest
19: Hannari_eli/Shutterstock
23: My Character/Shutterstock
25: Timur1985/Shutterstock
30: bangoland/Shutterstock
34: grinvalds/iStock
36: Walt Disney Studios Motion Pictures/Photofest
40: Streamline Pictures/Photofest
42: Sirichai Rattanaphanakul/Shutterstock
46: Colleen Michaels/Alamy Stock Photo
50: Sean Pavone/Shutterstock
52: ZUMA Press, Inc./Alamy Stock Photo
56: Valentina Szabo/Alamy Stock Photo

---

LIBRARY OF CONGRESS CATALOGING-IN-PUBLICATION DATA

Names: Kallen, Stuart A., 1955- author.
Title: Manga world / by Stuart A. Kallen.
Description: San Diego, CA : ReferencePoint Press, Inc., 2023. | Series: All things anime and manga | Includes bibliographical references and index.
Identifiers: LCCN 2022048698 (print) | LCCN 2022048699 (ebook) | ISBN 9781678205225 (library binding) | ISBN 9781678205232 (ebook)
Subjects: LCSH: Manga (Comic books)--Juvenile literature. | LCGFT: Comics criticism.
Classification: LCC PN6710 .K266 2023 (print) | LCC PN6710 (ebook) | DDC 741.5/9--dc23/eng/20221205
LC record available at https://lccn.loc.gov/2022048698
LC ebook record available at https://lccn.loc.gov/2022048699

# CONTENTS

**INTRODUCTION**    **4**
The World Loves Manga

**CHAPTER ONE**    **8**
The Evolution of Manga

**CHAPTER TWO**    **18**
Manga for Everyone

**CHAPTER THREE**    **28**
Reinventing Manga

**CHAPTER FOUR**    **38**
From Manga to Anime

**CHAPTER FIVE**    **48**
Cosplay Culture

| | |
|---|---|
| **Source Notes** | 58 |
| **For Further Research** | 61 |
| **Index** | 63 |

## INTRODUCTION

# THE WORLD LOVES MANGA

When the COVID-19 pandemic struck in early 2020, quarantine requirements forced bookstores and comic book shops to shut down in cities throughout the world. Publishers of manga, or Japanese comic books, feared sales would plunge. But something unexpected happened. People who were stuck at home started buying manga online in record numbers. And the buying binge continued into 2021 according to Lianne Sentar, sales manager at manga publisher Seven Seas Entertainment: "2021 numbers are off the charts. . . . We've truly never seen numbers like these."[1]

In 2022 manga publishers continued to use terms like *off the charts*, *explosive growth*, and *unprecedented* when describing sales. Much of this growth was fueled by younger readers who discovered animated Japanese cartoons, or anime, during the pandemic. Most anime is based on printed manga. After watching anime on sites like Crunchyroll and Netflix, viewers purchased the manga where the stories first appeared. This helped boost sales of older manga titles like *Fruits Basket*, *Attack on Titan*, and *Dragon Ball*, which were first published ten or even twenty years earlier. These developments helped the Japanese manga industry earn a record $5.7 billion in 2021.

And people throughout the world are still showing their love for manga, as Ed Chavez of DENPA publishing company says: "We're seeing lots of new [readers] from Southeast Asia, Philippines, India, Australia and New Zealand . . . even [the United Kingdom]."[2]

## UNIVERSAL THEMES

While interest in manga is soaring, sales figures do not tell the entire story. With the popularity of manga growing every year, a new wave of creative young artists is turning to digital publishing as a way to get their work in front of fans. While a few large companies in Japan control the manga publishing business, storytellers in South Korea, China, North America, and elsewhere are publishing their work on dedicated mobile apps like Comixology, INKR, Tapas, and Webtoon. Some have created characters based on their own racial heritage and sexual orientation. This allows the artists to cover issues such as prejudice, homophobia, transphobia, and other sensitive topics rarely covered in traditional manga stories.

While the stories might be coming from new perspectives, most tend to feature basic plotlines typical to all manga. Young heroes start out as struggling outcasts. They acquire magical or superhuman powers, expose injustice, fight evil, and find romance. When the characters transcend their mundane lives, they come to better understand themselves.

When manga artists focus on universal themes like friendship, love, and the struggle to fit in, they appeal to values held by their readers. And highlighting the interests and concerns of young people can lead to great success. Few *mangaka* (manga artists) grasp this dynamic better than Eiichiro Oda, who first published *One Piece*, the best-selling manga of all time, in 1997. The action-adventure story about a lovable pirate, Monkey D. Luffy, is still going strong today. Oda's success can be traced to the way he relates to his audience. He says, "Whenever I draw manga, I have only one reader in my mind—myself as a 15-year-old. . . . I turn back to the 15-year-old me to make a judgment on what is awesome or not. I always try to stay true to myself, and somehow it resonates with the kids who read my manga."3

## BUILDING BRIDGES

Although Japanese young adults are the largest group of manga consumers, manga has attracted devoted fans worldwide. Manga and anime pioneer Osamu Tezuka once explained his view of why this is so: "Comics are an international language, they can cross boundaries and generations. Comics are a bridge between all cultures."4 But in some ways it is surprising that manga built a bridge to Western culture. The Japanese manga format poses a

Manga are very different from most American comic books. Panel sequences unfold from right to left, and manga are often more than three hundred fifty pages and printed in black and white. Despite these differences, manga have attracted devoted fans worldwide.

challenge to readers raised on full-color, thirty-two-page American comic books. Most manga are printed in black and white, and panel sequences unfold from right to left, or "backward," on the page. And some manga magazines are as thick as books, with more than three hundred fifty pages. But readers love the endless parade of manga demon slayers, armor-plated alchemists, magical super-girls, frightening soul reapers, and talking cats.

Tezuka, who died in 1989, never lived to see manga grow into the worldwide phenomenon it has become. But it is easy to see that his prophetic words ring true. In the 2020s mangaka are spinning out creations in nearly every country on earth, including Brazil, China, France, Indonesia, Iran, Mexico, Turkey, and the United States. Many of the creators are inspired by their own personal experiences. And the stories often highlight ideas that can break down barriers between genders, generations, and cultures. In this way manga builds bridges that connect readers while helping them see the world in a new and different light.

> "Whenever I draw manga, I have only one reader in my mind—myself as a 15-year-old. . . . I always try to stay true to myself, and somehow it resonates with the kids who read my manga."[3]
>
> —Eiichiro Oda, mangaka

## CHAPTER ONE

# THE EVOLUTION OF MANGA

Manga is a big business in Japan, but it is much more than an industry. Since the 1980s manga has been at the center of what journalist Doug McGray calls "Japan's gross national cool."[5] The unique style of Japanese cool, which originates on the pages of manga magazines, can be seen in street fashion, music, theater, advertising, and graphic arts. Characters like Sailor Moon, Astro Boy, and Doraemon have become superstars in books, video games, live-action movies, and animated cartoons called anime.

While the manga industry helped transform Japanese popular culture, the drawing style is based on an ancient art tradition. According to American manga expert Frederik L. Schodt, "Japanese people have had a long love affair with art (especially monochromatic line drawings) that is fantastic, humorous, erotic, and sometimes violent."[6] The love of single-color, or monochromatic, drawings goes back to at least the 1800s, when mass-produced drawings hung on the walls of almost every shop and home in Japan.

In the nineteenth century, when Tokyo was known as Edo, average citizens struggled to survive. Families of merchants and laborers lived in tenement apartments not much bigger than modern jail cells. To escape their cramped quarters, Edo citizens visited *akusho*, or "bad places," such as theaters, teahouses, bars, and houses of prostitution in a huge red-light district called Yoshiwara. Because this area was a place where people could separate themselves from their harsh daily lives, it was commonly known as the "floating world," or *ukiyo*.

The activities of men and women in ukiyo inspired a type of popular art called floating world pictures, or *ukiyo-e*. Ukiyo-e featured scenes from nature, sword-wielding samurai warriors, and beautiful female entertainers known as geishas. These multicolor pictures were mass-produced with woodblock printing. Artisans carved the images into wooden blocks, which were coated with colored ink and pressed onto paper, like large stamps. The process allowed printers to create thousands of images from a single block, and the pictures spread quickly throughout society.

Katsushika Hokusai was one of the most renowned ukiyo-e artists in Edo. Hokusai published a fifteen-volume collection of his drawings called *Hokusai Manga* in 1814. The books contained four thousand sketches of plants, animals, ocean waves, mountains, and supernatural creatures such as gnomes and monsters. These sketches were among the first to be described as manga.

The Wave *is a famous print created in 1831 by Japanese artist Katsushika Hokusai. Hokusai published a collection of sketches that was among the first to be described as manga.*

> "[Traditional Japanese art called] ukiyo-e . . . was cheap to produce, widely circulated, and consistent with the spirit of play or entertainment."[7]
>
> —Sheri Le and Will Dodds, manga journalists

There are striking similarities between modern manga and the ukiyo-e by Hokusai and others of this era. According to manga journalists Sheri Le and Will Dodds, "[Ukiyo-e] artists often focused less on realistic artistic elements and more on introducing humor, eroticism, puzzles, and experiments with line and design to their work. Akin to the manga of today, ukiyo-e . . . was cheap to produce, widely circulated, and consistent with the spirit of play or entertainment."[7]

## WESTERN COMICS COME TO JAPAN

In the late nineteenth century, ukiyo-e artists found inspiration in another form of inexpensive illustrations that were circulating in American newspapers. Known as cartoons, comics, or funnies, these humorous drawings often poked fun at self-important people in what was called respectable society. One of the most popular American comics, *Hogan's Alley* by artist R.F. Outcault, first ran in the *New York World* in 1895. The comic featured a mischievous group of kids living in New York's extensive slums. The wry observations of the characters mocked the class and racial tensions that marked life in the city. The star of *Hogan's Alley* was a bald, bucktoothed character called the Yellow Kid who wore a yellow, oversized nightshirt.

The graphic design of *Hogan's Alley* was unique for the era. The comic was one of the first to feature four or five panels in a sequence. While earlier comics had text below the images, characters in *Hogan's Alley* expressed themselves in word balloons or speech bubbles that appeared above their heads. And the comic was printed in full color, a wonder of modern technology for the era. These features helped make *Hogan's Alley* extremely popular. According to comics historian Bill Blackbeard, "The Yellow Kid was the first great newspaper comic character in history."[8] This led to a marketing bonanza that would be familiar to fans of manga. The Yellow Kid was featured in plays and theatrical skits and used to sell a range of products that included chewing gum, dolls, postcards, and even whiskey and cigars.

By the 1920s American comic strip characters like the Yellow Kid, Little Orphan Annie, and Felix the Cat were as well known in Tokyo as they were in Tulsa. One of the most popular American comics, *Bringing Up Father* by George McManus, featured an Irish American named Jiggs, a former bricklayer, and his wife, Maggie, an ex-laundress. Jiggs achieves sudden wealth after winning the Irish Sweepstakes lottery. While Jiggs tries to stick to his uncouth, hard-partying ways, Maggie constantly berates him, hoping to make him more acceptable to polite society.

*Bringing Up Father* was immensely popular in Japan. In 1923 cartoonist Yutaka Asō was inspired to create a Japanese version of the comic called *Easygoing Daddy*. It featured a lazy father who reluctantly takes on odd jobs. The comic was an instant success. Like the Yellow Kid, Easygoing Daddy was used to sell a range of merchandise, including dolls and puppets. In later years the character was a star of books, radio shows, and movies.

## WHIMSICAL PICTURES

Sketches were first referred to as *manga* more than two hundred years ago, when renowned Japanese artist Katsushika Hokusai popularized the term in 1814. At the time *manga* was commonly interpreted to mean "whimsical pictures." But the word has a deeper meaning. As Asian art expert Jocelyn Bouquillard explains, the written Japanese symbol for *manga* denotes spontaneous drawings made by an artist who is "incoherent, disjointed, confused, or casual." Bouquillard writes that the symbol "suggests rough, rapid sketches—impromptu drawings done on the tide of inspiration, freely and with no sense of order, on a variety of subjects."

Hokusai's drawings, which largely consisted of people, animals, and nature scenes, would never be confused for modern manga. The term was first used to describe cartoons and comic strips around 1902. Credit goes to Japanese artist Rakuten Kitazawa, who published his work in a color cartoon magazine called *Tokyo Puck*. The magazine, which soon had a circulation of more than one hundred thousand, helped make Kitazawa rich and famous. And his quickly created, whimsical pictures helped popularize the term *manga* as it is understood today.

Jocelyn Bouquillard and Christophe Marquet, *Hokusai: The First Manga Master*. New York: Abrams, 2007, p. 9.

## OSAMU TEZUKA'S MANGA MAKEOVER

From 1941 to 1945 Japan and the United States fought each other in World War II. The war ended shortly after the United States dropped atomic bombs on two Japanese cities, Hiroshima and Nagasaki. During the postwar period that followed, people in Japan were hungry and demoralized. Death had touched nearly every family. In this atmosphere, people wanted inexpensive entertainment that would help them forget their troubles. Eighteen-year-old artist Osamu Tezuka was there to provide relief.

Tezuka was fascinated by the cheap comic books sold in market stalls. These books were called *akahon*, or "red books," named for the bright red and orange ink used on covers to attract children. Red books were printed on cheap paper by small publishers who hired young artists desperate for work. In 1947 Tezuka was one of those artists; he and others were willing to

Osamu Tezuka's Mighty Atom, pictured here, became a national icon in Japan and was the star of the country's first anime television series of the same name. The series was later renamed *Astro Boy* and broadcast in the United States.

toil day and night to launch their careers. Tezuka produced hundreds of drawings for a comic called *New Treasure Island*. The story followed a boy named Pete who finds a treasure map, sails off in pursuit of riches, and experiences a series of misfortunes. When it was published Tezuka became an overnight sensation. While many Japanese people barely had enough money for food, *New Treasure Island* quickly sold over four hundred thousand copies.

> "I made a point of depicting a movement or facial expression with many frames, even many pages. The result was a super-long comic."[9]
>
> —Osamu Tezuka, mangaka

*New Treasure Island* was unlike any previously published comic book. At the time most Japanese comics were short and portrayed flat figures in square boxes. *New Treasure Island* weighed in at a book-length 190 pages. The drawings were cinematic, with panels that unfolded like scenes in a movie. Tezuka created scenes that zoomed in from a distance to extreme close-ups that might show only lines of emotion in a character's eyes and forehead. A series of wide panels that took in an entire landscape were reminiscent of a movie camera panning from side to side. Another technique showed the action from above, from below, and from unusual angles. These panels resembled quick cuts in a film that add tension and excitement.

Tezuka deliberately broke with the past when he created *New Treasure Island*. He felt that traditional comics, which were drawn as if an audience was viewing the action on a stage, were stale and boring. Tezuka explained:

This [old style of drawing] made it impossible to create dramatic or psychological effects, so I began to use cinematic techniques. . . . I experimented with close-ups and different angles, and instead of using only one frame for an action scene or the climax (as was customary), I made a point of depicting a movement or facial expression with many frames, even many pages. The result was a super-long comic.[9]

# ASTRO BOY FLIES OFF THE PAGE

After the success of *New Treasure Island*, Tezuka created thousands of pages of manga, including historical works, detective stories, romances, and science fiction. Whatever the genre of the story, Tezuka's work often contained subject matter concerning peace and environmentalism. He was moved to explore these themes after seeing the horrifying effects of war and the devastation caused by the atomic bombs. Through his work, Tezuka came to believe that he could convince people to coexist peacefully and take care of the planet. As Schodt explains, "[Tezuka's] revulsion for war [was] a theme that would permeate nearly all the works he later created. Moreover, he developed a lifelong interest in the complexity of human nature, a deep belief in the need to communicate with other cultures, and a belief in the power of manga and animation to help do so."[10]

> "[Osamu Tezuka developed] a deep belief in the need to communicate with other cultures, and a belief in the power of manga and animation to help do so."[10]
>
> —Frederik L. Schodt, American manga expert

Tezuka's most iconic character, Tetsuwan Atomu (Mighty Atom in English), reflects the artist's desire to promote peace. Tezuka created the Mighty Atom, a boy robot with superpowers, in 1952. The Mighty Atom was built by a mad scientist in what was then the distant future, April 7, 2003. The futuristic Mighty Atom had a nuclear reactor heart, a computer brain, searchlight eyes, a machine gun in his backside, lasers in his hands, and rockets in his feet, which allow him to fly through the air. He was able to understand sixty languages, had super hearing and vision, and could smash through concrete with his 100,000-horsepower strength. Despite his awesome powers, the Mighty Atom was also cute and cuddly.

The Mighty Atom appeared in manga series for sixteen years while becoming a national icon in Japan. In 1963 the character starred in Japan's first anime television series, which was retitled *Astro Boy* and broadcast in the United States. This achievement helped make Tezuka one of the most influential mangaka in histo-

## THE APPEAL OF SAILOR MOON

When the English-language version of the *Sailor Moon* manga by Naoko Takeuchi first appeared in the United States in 1997, young female readers instantly took to the series. Sailor Moon and her Sailor Guardians are tough, beautiful, and elegant but they also act like ordinary teenagers. They hang out, eat pizza, play video games, and chase boys. But when evil looms, the crime-fighting Sailor Guardians come together to fight that threat.

Manga journalist Jessica Lord explains why the series has been so popular. She writes that Sailor Moon "teaches girls to be proud of who they are, find power in their femininity, and make choices that build healthy relationships. All that coupled with action and romance makes Sailor Moon an amazing series that offers a lot to its target audience. And that's more than can be said for most media aimed at young girls."

Jessica Lord, "Sailor Moon: Positive Female Role Model Since 1992," Tofugu, May 5, 2014. www .tofugu.com.

---

ry. The large eyes, button noses, and other characteristic features of his creations have been imitated by almost every mangaka in the past sixty years. Tezuka's thrilling cinematic drawings, combined with long, inventive stories, made readers almost feel as if they were watching a film. And the way he portrayed action on the page has been described as a hybrid of manga and anime. Little wonder that Tezuka is still referred to today as a *manga no kami*—literally "god of comics."

## SAILOR MOON *COMES TO AMERICA*

At the time of his death in 1989, Tezuka's work was virtually unknown in the United States. But Seiji Horibuchi, a Japanese immigrant in California, was working to change that. Horibuchi launched Viz Media in 1986 to introduce American readers to manga. Within a year, the company released its first manga, an English-language version of the samurai action title *Lone Wolf and Cub*. In order to attract an American audience, Viz printed the pages "flopped." They were meant to be read from left to right, unlike the right-to-left format of Japanese manga. At the time, flopped manga that was translated into English was referred to as Amerimanga.

This picture shows the main characters of Sailor Moon, a manga series that was later adapted into an anime series and quickly became an American pop culture sensation. The story follows a team of schoolgirls who transform into crime-fighting superheroes.

The violent, edgy *Lone Wolf and Cub*, aimed at older male readers, sold one hundred thousand copies in the United States. Despite the success, sales of Amerimanga languished. It took a group of magical girls in *Sailor Moon* to make Japanese manga an American pop culture sensation. *Sailor Moon* first appeared in manga in 1991. The story follows a schoolgirl named Usagi Tsukino, who transforms into a girl with magical powers called Sailor Moon. She assembles a team, the Sailor Guardians, who can change from normal schoolgirls into crime-fighting heroes with supernatural powers. The Sailor Guardians battle dark forces from outer space, monsters from another dimension, and wicked life-forms bent on destroying the universe.

*Sailor Moon* was adapted into an anime series in Japan in 1992. An English-language version of the *Sailor Moon* anime began running on the USA cable network in 1996. The show quickly found a dedicated audience of female American fans. The sixty original chapters of the *Sailor Moon* manga were serialized, or produced in a series, until 1997. The manga was one of the most successful and influential of all time.

*Sailor Moon* has been credited with launching the manga mania that shows no signs of slowing in the twenty-first century. This worldwide phenomenon with roots in ancient Japanese art and American comic strips has had an impact that cannot be denied. Manga has evolved into one of the most influential forms of entertainment in the modern world, and it will undoubtedly continue to amuse and amaze for decades to come.

## CHAPTER TWO

# MANGA FOR EVERYONE

One reason manga is so popular is that fans can find stories for almost every taste, interest, and age group. But keeping up with all of the different manga is pretty much impossible. According to a publishing trade group in Japan, around 8,000 manga titles are printed every year—more than 150 each week. The dizzying array of manga titles includes cutesy kid's stuff like *Pokémon Adventures*, love stories such as *Skip Beat!*, and the ultraviolent *Chainsaw Man*.

Outside of Japan, publishing houses in South Korea, the United States, and elsewhere put out thousands of other manga titles. And independent mangaka upload countless manga to digital sites every day. This mountain of manga can be broken down into dozens of genres and subgenres, including comedy, sports, romance, fantasy, science fiction, and the supernatural. But most manga, wherever it is created, fits into five broad genres. These categories were devised long ago when publishers in Japan produced manga for specific demographic groups defined by age and gender.

## KODOMO MANGA FOR YOUNG READERS

The worldwide success of manga has its roots in a basic tenet of the entertainment business: There are billions of dollars to be made by creating content for kids. In Japan interest in manga starts at an early age. Most children are given *kodomo* manga as soon as they can read, or even before.

The term *kodomo* comes from *kodomomuke*, which means "intended for children." Most of the manga in this category is created for kids under age ten. The genre is the oldest of any manga category; the first printed kodomo magazines appeared in the late 1800s. These publications were around fifteen pages long and were meant to encourage literacy while simultaneously entertaining young readers. The manga were one-offs—they were single stories, not part of a multivolume series. Most kodomo manga ended with simple lessons such as instructing readers to eat their vegetables or wash their hands. In the 1920s the magazine *Kodomo no kuni*, or "Land of Children," established a higher standard of quality for children's publications. The magazine published artistic manga with original stories meant to encourage learning and creativity.

*Thousands of manga titles are printed every year, with stories for almost every taste, interest, and age group.* Pokémon Adventures, *pictured here, is popular with children.*

Kodomo manga was little known outside Japan until a blue robot cat named Doraemon became a worldwide cultural icon. *Doraemon*, which roughly translates as "stray cat," was initially created in 1969 by Hiroshi Fujimoto and Motoo Abiko, who worked together under the pen name Fujiko Fujio. *Doraemon* follows a time-traveling feline from the twenty-second century. The cat returns to the twentieth century to help a bumbling, bullied ten-year-old schoolboy named Nobita Nobi. And Nobita needs all the help he can get; he is weak, useless at sports, and a lazy student who gets bad grades. Doraemon's mission is to help Nobita find success so that his descendants can have better lives in the future. To accomplish this goal, Doraemon uses a wide array of futuristic gadgets meant to help Nobita in any crisis. The tools include the Anywhere Door, which transports

## ROOTS OF KODOMO MANGA

Kodomo manga like *Doraemon* and *Pokémon* are known throughout the world. These series created for kids under ten can trace their roots back to the 1920s, an era known as the golden age of Japanese children's manga. The era of artistic excellence began in 1922 with the founding of the magazine *Kodomo no kuni*, or "Land of Children." *Kodomo no kuni* hired renowned artists and illustrators, along with child psychologists, poets, and songwriters. These experts produced high-quality stories meant to educate and amuse. Between the covers of kodomo manga, readers could find literary manga stories, illustrated dance lessons, craft instruction, and songs complete with musical notation. Art expert Tara M. McGowan describes the cultural impact of *Kodomo no kuni*:

[Artists] did not just depict the children they saw around them, they reimagined and redefined a fashionable and active lifestyle for educated children of the urban middle-class. In *Kodomo no kuni*, children are often shown in charge of themselves and empowered to take control of their modern, urban surroundings. . . . Along with physical freedom and agency in their modern setting, the magazine encouraged children's freedom of expression through various arts competitions. Winning entries would often be published at the end of the volumes.

Tara M. McGowan, "Welcome to the 'Land of Children' (*Kodomo no kuni*): Courtesy of a Gift from the Friends of Princeton University Library," Princeton University Library, February 1, 2019. https://blogs.princeton.edu.

people to various locations depending on their thoughts, and the Take-Copter, a small helicopter-like device worn as a hat that allows users to fly.

*Doraemon* was first serialized in children's monthly magazines aimed at kids ages four to eight. But during its thirty-year run, the series went on to become the most popular manga in Japan, selling over 108 million paperback books called *tankōbon* that contain multiple chapters of a single series. Doraemon continued to appear in over forty feature-length anime; the most recent, *Doraemon: Nobita's New Dinosaur*, was released in 2020. The manga also spawned several theatrical musicals, numerous video games, and three separate anime television series that total more than sixteen hundred episodes.

## SHONEN MANGA FOR BOYS

*Doraemon* is one of the biggest names in Japanese pop culture, despite the fact that it was created for a grade-school audience. But there are many other manga icons in Japan, and most come out of a genre known as *shonen* manga, which caters to boys ages twelve to eighteen. *Shonen*, also spelled *shōnen* or *shounen*, means "young male" in Japanese.

Shonen is the largest, most profitable manga genre. And this style has been a driving force behind the manga industry since the magazine *Shōnen Club* was first printed in Japan in 1914. In the 1930s *Shōnen Club* devised the iconic format that is still widely used today in the numerous weekly manga magazines. *Shōnen Club* had four hundred pages and featured beautifully illustrated black-and-white comics. Most stories were serialized with a new chapter appearing in each issue. Today this format can be seen in the most popular manga magazines in Japan, including *Weekly Shōnen Jump* and *Weekly Shōnen Magazine*.

Like the format, the basic plot points of shonen manga stories have changed little over the decades. Most tales feature a young central character, or protagonist, who sets out on a personal quest. The manga heroes often have to defeat vicious enemies while confronting their own personal weaknesses. They must master their emotions, overcome physical and mental limitations, and grow and mature. These recurring themes fit easily into the most popular shonen manga genres, which include supernatural, martial arts, sports, fantasy, and science fiction.

Manga journalist Jessica Roar explains the appeal of these themes to tweens and teens: "Shounen [stories] often go on for long periods of time and feature lots of fighting. Most of the characters in shounen are young males who set out . . . to fulfill their dreams. In this genre, you will find characters you can grow up with."[11] These characters have appeared in dozens of best-selling shonen manga stories. They include Shinichi Kudō, the exceptional young detective in *Case Closed* who was transformed into a child after being poisoned. Kudō has been entertaining shonen fans since 1994 and continues to do so today in manga, anime, video games, music, books, and live-action films.

Like Kudō, many other characters first achieved popularity in shonen manga and went on to become entertainment superstars. They include the young ninja fighter Naruto Uzumaki from *Naruto*; Gon Freecss, the protagonist from *Hunter x Hunter*; and the high school student Yuji Itadori, who kicks and slashes against evil in *Jujutsu Kaisen*.

While these and other shonen manga target tweens and teens, the stories have universal appeal. Westerners traveling in Japan often marvel at the sight of grown men on commuter trains absorbed in the latest shonen manga. Comics promoter Paul Gravett offers his explanation for this phenomenon: "What seems to sell *Shōnen Jump* and other titles to boys of six to 60 is their values of friendship, perseverance—and winning. . . . The Japanese have continued to find inspiration and solace in shonen manga heroes. It's somehow fitting that that word *shonen* . . . [is] made up of the [Japanese alphabet] characters for "few" and "years," but also "pure of heart.""[12]

> "What seems to sell *Shōnen Jump* and other [manga] titles to boys of six to 60 is their values of friendship, perseverance—and winning."[12]
>
> —Paul Gravett, comics promoter

Naruto *is an anime and manga series that follows a young ninja fighter named Naruto Uzumaki (pictured), who dreams of becoming the leader of his village.*

### SHOJO MANGA FOR GIRLS

Shonen manga stories often focus on buddies, bravery, and conquest, but the genre rarely highlights romance. Shonen manga relationships are often superficial; love and affection are secondary to the hero's desire to achieve his goals and vanquish his enemies. Sometimes, love affairs are used to inject humor in a story; oftentimes, protagonists are amusingly oblivious to the romantic advances of attractive young women.

While romance might be a subplot in shonen manga, it tends to be central to most *shojo* manga. *Shojo*, also spelled *shōjo* or *shoujo*, translates to "young girl" and is aimed at female readers ages twelve to eighteen. The origins of the genre can be traced to 1923, when the publisher of *Shōnen Club* introduced *Shōjo Club*. While shojo manga were popular among Japanese girls, most were written and illustrated by men. They often featured unoriginal romance stories filled with lonely tomboys or unloved waifs who could only find happiness through marriage. This changed in the early 1970s, when popular magazines like *Shōjo Comic* and *Best Friend* began hiring female mangaka. Many of the new artists were in their early twenties (or around twenty-four years old). Newspaper articles about the rise of female mangaka referred to the new generation of women artists as the *Showa 24* (Year 24) or the Magnificent 24s. The Magnificent 24s includes a group of venerated Japanese artists such

## A DIFFERENT VIEW ON THE PAGE

In the 1970s women artists made stylistic changes to shojo manga to make it more appealing to female readers. While male artists drew square, linear panels, women went beyond the rectangular boundaries, as comics promoter Paul Gravett explains:

Men's logic and linearity were overruled. The generation of female mangaka unchained their panels from the uniformly regimented rectangles and rows beloved of the male creators. They gave their panels whatever shape and configuration best suited the emotions they wanted to evoke. They softened the ruled borders outlining their panels, sometimes breaking them up, dissolving them or removing them all together. They overlapped or merged sequences of panels into collages. A borderless panel could now permeate the page, often beneath flotillas of other panels sailing across it, or it could expand or "bleed" off the edges of the printed page itself and imply an even bigger picture beyond the paper. Thus time and reality were no longer always locked up inside boxes and narratives could shift in and out of memories and dreams. Characters too were no longer always contained within panels, but could stand in front of them, sometimes shown in full length.

Paul Gravett, *Manga: Sixty Years of Japanese Comics*. New York: Harper Design International, 2004, p. 79.

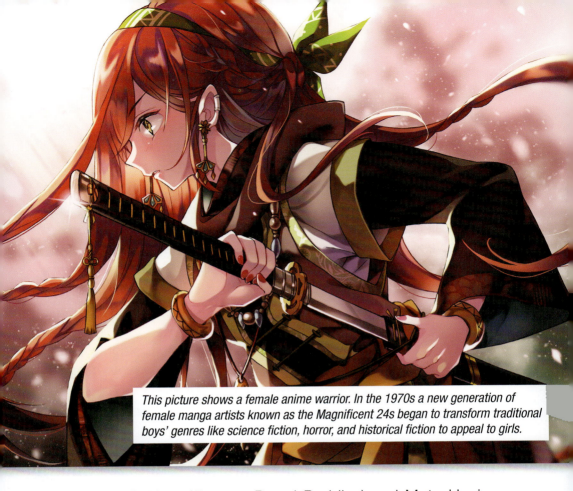

This picture shows a female anime warrior. In the 1970s a new generation of female manga artists known as the Magnificent 24s began to transform traditional boys' genres like science fiction, horror, and historical fiction to appeal to girls.

as Yumiko Oshima (*Banana Bread Pudding*) and Moto Hagio (*They Were Eleven*).

The Magnificent 24s increased shojo manga sales by breaking barriers. The female mangaka transformed traditional boys' genres like science fiction, horror, and historical fiction to appeal to female sensibilities. This meant toning down the violence while presenting plots that developed at a slower pace. These changes were presented in an artistic style that was seen as more appealing to the feminine eye. Rather than using rectangular panels typically seen in shonen manga, female mangaka used panels of different shapes and sizes to highlight drama or action.

The changes instituted by the Magnificent 24s are still seen in shojo manga today. Stories tend to focus on relationships, moods, daydreams, and longings. Characters often have huge, round,

> "The eyes literally are the windows of the soul; by looking at the eyes, the readers can intuit the character's feelings, which remain unexpressed in dialog."[13]
>
> —Mizuki Takahashi, Japanese art and culture expert

doll-like eyes that can take up half of the character's extremely large head, which itself might fill the entire page. This drawing style shows subtle expressions that demonstrate a character's inner thoughts, intimate feelings, and psychological makeup. According to Japanese art and culture expert Mizuki Takahashi, "The aesthetic features, such as enormous eyes with long eyelashes, full-body portraits, and complicated panel designs are crucial for fans to engage emotionally with the story. . . . [The eyes] serve as mirrors that reflect the character's emotions. In other words, the eyes literally are the windows of the soul; by looking at the eyes, the readers can intuit the character's feelings, which remain unexpressed in dialog."[13]

As might be expected, most shojo manga protagonists are young women. They are often torn between finding love and the need to carry out important tasks. As with shonen manga characters, leading characters are usually outsiders who accidentally fall into a world of dramatic adventure. The main character is usually surrounded by a gang of girlfriends who fit into various stereotypes; one is smart, one is beautiful, one is funny, and one is scatterbrained.

## MANY SUBGENRES

Some shojo manga stories explore formerly taboo subjects such as incest, drug addiction, suicide, and divorce. Others focus on nontraditional notions of gender and sexuality. Homosexuality, in particular, was unmentionable in the world of manga. But the Magnificent 24s and other female mangaka were fearless when it came to exploring the sexuality of characters. So many manga series were created with gay characters that the topic is no longer considered shocking. Stories focusing on homosexual romances have become so common in mainstream shojo that the genre is simply referred to as "boys' love" and "girls' love."

Another popular character type seen in shojo manga is the androgynous "beautiful boy" who resembles a girl. As East Asian studies professor Jennifer Prough writes, "It is often hard for the uninitiated to identify these beautiful boys as male characters—their hair typically long and flowing, their waists are narrow, their legs long, and their eyes big in shōjo manga style."[14]

Shojo manga can be broken down into other subgenres, including school life, humor, fantasy, adventure, drama, romance, and slice of life. Some stories include one or two subgenres, while others might have more. For example, the manga series *No Longer Heroine* by Momoko Koda is about a teenager named Hatori who believed she would marry the boy of her dreams. But the boy was interested in another girl. The story, released in English in 2022, features love triangles, competition with beautiful rivals, emotional confessions, and some comedic scenes. With these varying aspects, the story is classified in the subgenres of comedy, drama, romance, school life, and slice of life.

The series *The Saint's Magic Power Is Omnipotent* is an adventure/fantasy romance that tells the story of Aira Misono, an ordinary high school girl who was reincarnated as a supposed saint. Aira needs to save the world from monsters but must compete with another woman who is an actual saint. And of course there is a romantic angle involving a handsome prince. The manga, written by Yuka Tachibana and illustrated by Fujiazuki, was serialized from 2018 to 2021 and received an anime adaptation in 2021.

As with shojo, shonen manga can also fit into several subgenres that include sports, crime, and comedy. With a wild profusion of genres, subgenres, and sub-subgenres, the never-ending cascade of manga can fuel the imagination of anyone, whatever their age, gender, taste, or preference.

## CHAPTER THREE

# REINVENTING MANGA

Readers who are new to the world of manga are often confused by the crazy profusion of stories, series, and genres produced in Japan. If they enjoy manga online, they might also be perplexed by the terms used to describe digital manga. Digital Japanese manga are called webcomics, and they have a specific format. Webcomics are made to be viewed on a computer, tablet, or smartphone. They appear on-screen as printed manga magazines with multiple frames of black-and-white drawings on each page. Readers flip through the pages as if they were reading a digital book.

Japan long ruled the world of online webcomics. But when K-pop music became an international phenomenon in the 2010s, interest in South Korean pop culture spiked. Hoping to learn more about the culture that gave birth to K-pop, fans worldwide began reading South Korean manga, called *manhwa*. Millions used the Webtoon app, which was already trendy in South Korea.

The digitally formatted manhwa on Webtoon look different; stories are specifically designed to be enjoyed on small smartphone screens. Instead of flipping pages, readers scroll down through long, vertical strips consisting of single panels. Most drawings are in color and feature easy-to-read large text. Some even provide soundtracks and animation to heighten the reading experience. Blogger Kadi Yao Tay praises the Webtoon format: "The infinite, vertical scrolling format is awesome for reading comics on the go. No need to pinch to zoom, or scan over a page repeatedly to capture all the details. The inclusion of animation and music make for exciting and interactive reading. For reading on tiny screens, this format is perfect."[15]

> "[Webtoon's] infinite, vertical scrolling format is awesome for reading comics on the go. . . . The inclusion of animation and music make for exciting and interactive reading."[15]
>
> —Kadi Yao Tay, blogger

Webtoon was launched by South Korean publishing giant Naver Corporation in 2004. Webtoon began offering South Korean manhwa translated into English in 2014. By 2022 the platform had 82 million active monthly users, with 15 million in the United States, according to company statistics. As artist Tae Yim explains, "It's a younger medium but fast-growing, especially in the US."[16] The site is so popular that many fans now refer to all scrolling-style manhwa as webtoons, even if they appear on other popular South Korean sites such as Manta Comics, Netcomics, and Toomics.

## RACHEL SMYTHE'S LORE

South Korean webtoons platforms are particularly popular with creators. While it is nearly impossible to break into the highly competitive manga industry in Japan, sites like Webtoon allow anyone to post their work. Those who build a loyal following can earn income through donations and subscriptions. And the format is attracting a new audience of Gen Z and millennial women; around half of Webtoon subscribers are female. This is largely due to the fact that many of the most popular webtoons are created by women, and not all of them are South Korean. Nothing illustrates this dynamic better than the notable success of New Zealand artist Rachel Smythe, one of around fifteen hundred English-language creators on Webtoon.

Smythe's *Lore Olympus* webtoon is a reimagining of the relationship between classical Greek deities. But it is set in the modern age of cars and smartphones. The main story follows the abduction of Persephone, the goddess of spring, by Hades, the god of the underworld. As award-winning cartoonist Faith Erin Hicks describes it, "*Lore Olympus* is an addictive, romantic gem of a comic, filled with complex, lovable (and hateable) characters. The artwork is rich and dramatic, with gorgeous colors and bold linework, each panel a dreamy treat for the eyes."[17]

*Lore Olympus* was a hit when Smythe first self-published it on Webtoon in 2018. By 2022 it was the most popular comic on the site, attracting more than 1.1 billion views and nearly 6 million subscribers. A print version of the webtoon, *Lore Olympus: Volume One*, reached number one on the *New York Times* bestseller list in 2021. Two more collected print volumes followed, and plans for a *Lore Olympus* anime were in the works in 2022.

Smythe won numerous awards, including the prestigious Will Eisner Comic Industry Award (commonly called the Eisner Award)

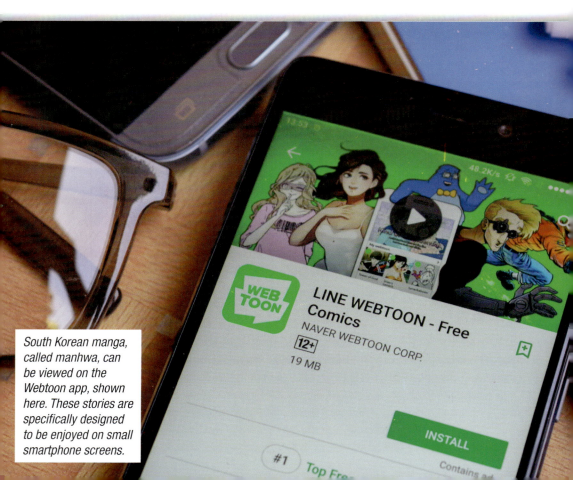

South Korean manga, called manhwa, can be viewed on the Webtoon app, shown here. These stories are specifically designed to be enjoyed on small smartphone screens.

in 2021 for Best Webcomic. Producing a weekly webtoon is incredibly demanding. Smythe says she works up to seventy hours a week, most of it drawing while hunched over a screen. But the work pays well. Smythe has earned millions of dollars as one of the premier Webtoon creators.

> "We're incredibly proud of the . . . ecosystem we've built to celebrate and support Webtoon creators."[18]
>
> —Ken Kim, chief executive officer of Webtoon North America

According to the Webtoon website, the company has paid artists over $27 million since 2020. And the chief executive officer of Webtoon North America, Ken Kim, is proud of his company's contribution to the comics industry. He says:

> Webtoon creators are some of the most talented, creative, and captivating in the history of comics. Our storytelling technology platform supports every type of creator, allowing them to build a global audience and make money from their work. In a time when comics have never been more popular, we're incredibly proud of the growing Creator Economy and ecosystem we've built to celebrate and support Webtoon creators.[18]

## A NEW TAKE ON MAGICAL GIRLS

While the Webtoon app grabs most of the attention in South Korea, there are alternative apps that present digital comics formatted for smartphones. The platform Tapas had over 1 million users in 2022, and the majority of them lived in North America. According to company statistics, more than 80 percent of Tapas readers are age seventeen to twenty-five, and around two-thirds are women.

Tapas fans love the app because it publishes stories that look at the world from a different perspective. One example, *Magical Boy* by Chicago native Vincent Kao, has been among the most popular webtoons on Tapas since it first appeared in 2018. While magical girls have been very popular since *Sailor Moon* first ap-

## A COMMUNITY FOR CREATORS

The digital publishing platform Tapas is committed to promoting the works made by independent manga artists. In 2021 this led the site to launch Tapastry, a forum for its fifty-eight thousand creators that allows them to communicate directly with readers. Artists can use Tapastry to share their personal stories while attracting new viewers to their webtoons. Tapastry publishes a newsletter, and followers can connect with creators in the forum on Twitter, Instagram, and Facebook. An unnamed Tapas representative describes the endeavor: "Just like countless individual unique threads being woven together to form one detailed picture, also called a tapestry, the Tapas creators have created a community that is unique in the publishing landscape. . . . Tapastry is actively working towards making it possible for creators to earn money with their craft."

Quoted in Adi Tantimedh, "Tapas Launches Tapastry, the Tapas Creator Community," Bleeding Cool, January 13, 2021. https://bleedingcool.com.

peared in the early 1990s, *Magical Boy* comes with a twist; it is about a transgender teenage boy named Max who was assigned female at birth. As Max deals with typical high school problems, he learns from his mother that he is a descendent of Aurora, the Roman goddess of light. The hilarious story follows Max as he fights to save humanity from an evil force, accompanied by a feisty feline and a gang of friends.

Kao, known as "the Kao" on Tapas, was born in 1992 and grew up reading popular shonen manga like *Dragon Ball Z*. But Kao says he could not relate to some of the stories because there were few gay or trans characters. He explains:

> *Magical Boy* was born from the simple idea and desire of wanting more trans representation in the media. I then incorporated my love for anime, such as *Sailor Moon*, to create this unique take on the magical girl genre. From there . . . I wanted to make sure that I was making Max's experience as authentic and relatable as I could. I spent a lot of time doing research by talking to my friends in the trans community, and by also watching YouTube vlogs by transmen who bravely shared their stories online.[19]

Kao says he was surprised when Tapas said it would back *Magical Boy* with funding and promotion. Most publishers tell artists that it is difficult to make money with LGBTQ+ story lines. But *Magical Boy* attracted so much attention that the story was adapted as a graphic novel in 2022. While some have tried to ban books and graphic novels about transgender issues from libraries, Tapas vice president of content Michael Son ignores the divisive politics. "The readers really directed what content directions we were taking,"[20] he says.

## BEGINNING SOMETHING NEW

Tapas readers tend to be young and female, and they love material with elements of fantasy and romance. This helped make *The Beginning After the End* webtoon another big hit on the app. The upbeat action/fantasy story, by two creators who go by the names TurtleMe and Fuyuki23, recorded 28 million views by 2022. *The Beginning After the End*, popularly known as *TBATE*, is what is known as an *isekai* story. This is a fantasy subgenre in which characters are suddenly transported from their familiar surroundings to an unknown world. In *TBATE* a ruler named King Grey comes back to life as Arthur Leywin, a boy who uses knowledge of his past life to become a gifted magician. *TBATE* was released as a printed graphic novel in 2021, prompting a statement from TurtleMe: "While the craft of storytelling has evolved alongside technology in order to be consumed on a screen instead of paper, it's a great honor to have my story printed and distributed on paper so that my beloved readers and myself can physically hold it and keep it as a part of our bookshelves."[21]

## AN INTERNATIONAL AUDIENCE

With webtoons attracting interest throughout the world, South Korean digital platforms are focusing on expanding their borders. In 2014 Naver Corporation founded LINE Webtoon in India. The South Korean titles on the site were translated into the two most

*This picture shows an animator using editing software to draw a portrait. Creating webtoons is very demanding, requiring hours of work every day.*

common languages used in India, Hindi and Telugu. One of the most popular webtoons on the site is *Brown Paperbag* by Sailesh Gopalan. The comic about growing up in India first appeared in 2016. By 2022 Gopalan had produced 155 episodes that attracted over 4 million views. Gopalan, who attended art school in Bangalore, India, loved to draw comics but never expected to achieve success. He offers this advice to aspiring creators: "Upload! Don't let your inhibitions keep you from sharing your work with the world. I had no idea my comics would receive the response it did, and the only way I could know is if I put it up on the Webtoon."[22]

The success of Webtoon in India inspired another South Korean company to launch an app there in 2020. Kross Komics offers digital comics in Hindi, Telugu, and English. The platform is designed to appeal to female readers ages fifteen to twenty-four who also enjoy South Korean television soap operas called K-drama. As Kross Komics cofounder Hyunwoo Thomas Kim explains, "The popularity of K-Pop and K-Drama has been growing exponentially in India in the last couple of years, and that has opened up Korean culture to many young Indian consumers. . . . Indians are now exposed to everything K [South Korean], including K-Beauty, K-Drama, K-Pop, so now they are ready to explore more and K-Webtoon is an interesting area."[23]

## AMERICANS JUMP INTO WEBTOONS

While the art featured in most digital comics follows traditional manga styles, that is set to change. Major American comic book publishers—including Marvel Comics, DC Comics, and Archie Comic Publications—are partnering with Webtoon. These industry

### SENSITIVE TRANSLATIONS

As with any manga, drawings are central to webtoons, but words also help tell the stories. Because online comics are available in over one hundred countries, translations are an important part of the product. Bad translations can ruin the artist's work. Translations have to be sensitive to local culture, slang, and jargon. The South Korean publishing giant Kakao—which provides digital comics to numerous countries, including France, Indonesia, Japan, Taiwan, and Thailand—is keenly aware that translations can make or break a series. Kakao employs what it calls global localization teams. These teams interpret language and cultural references to ensure they accurately reflect the meaning intended by the artists while avoiding unintentional gaffes. As team leader Lee Jae-won explains:

> Choosing the title is the first step in localization. Language usage in various countries, including the use of [synonyms], polite words, religion and other cultural factors, are carefully considered in the process of translating. . . . We aim to successfully deliver the creator's messages and intention with translations and graphic adaptations that are appropriate to each target country.

Quoted in Lee Si-Jin, "Korean Webtoons Expand Globally with Different Strategies," Asia News Network, September 7, 2022. https://asianews.network.

giants plan to produce original stories featuring renowned characters, including Spider-Man, Black Panther, Superman, and others.

The first major collaboration between DC and Webtoon in 2021 resulted in a reimagining of the iconic Batman character. *Batman: Wayne Family Adventures* is a slice-of-life comic. It offers laughs and a little drama by delving into what it calls a be-

The art in most digital comics follows traditional manga styles, however, that is likely to change soon. Major American comic book publishers are partnering with Webtoon and plan to produce original stories featuring renowned characters such as the Black Panther (pictured).

> **"It's safe to say, webtoons are the future of comics."[25]**
>
> —Tae Yim, webtoon artist

hind-the-mask look at the Bat Family. In this revamped series, all of Bruce Wayne's adopted, fostered, and biological superhero children are alive and battling evil while living under one roof in Wayne Manor. Characters include Jason Todd (Red Hood), Damian Wayne (Robin), and Barbara Gordon (Oracle), along with the wise butler, Alfred.

While there is some superhero action, *Batman: Wayne Family Adventures* delves into personal conflicts and the difficulties of achieving a work-life balance. As reviewer Lisa Fernandes writes, "The comic is just plain wonderful at reflecting the ups-and-downs of life while filling in missing moments and solving conflicts in a relatable way. And there's definitely some dashing heroics. . . . Readers won't find a better *Batman* comic on the market."[24] Readers agreed with Fernandes; *Batman: Wayne Family Adventures* was instantly popular, attracting over 165,000 subscribers within nine hours of its release. By 2022 the Webtoon Bat Family had attracted over 56 million views.

Old favorites like Batman might attract the most eyeballs on Webtoon. But millions more enjoy lesser-known comics created by a new generation of writers and illustrators. These creators from Albania to Zambia are attracting readers, reinventing manga, and finding unprecedented opportunities in the world of digital comics. And some are seeing their creations adapted into books, television dramas and comedies, anime, and even K-pop songs. With Webtoons and other digital comics becoming a globalized, multimedia phenomenon, the industry is expected to generate $26 billion annually by 2028. As Tae Yim observes, "It's safe to say, webtoons are the future of comics."[25]

# CHAPTER FOUR

# FROM MANGA TO ANIME

The worlds of manga and anime have been intertwined since *Mighty Atom* debuted on Japanese television in 1963. The animated cartoon, based on Osamu Tezuka's wildly popular manga series, was an instant hit in Japan. *Mighty Atom* was renamed *Astro Boy* when it was broadcast in the United States on Saturday morning television from 1963 to 1966. *Astro Boy* was soon joined on American TV by other Japanese anime series like *Speed Racer* and *Gigantor*. While the shows were popular, most viewers were unaware that they were watching anime created from extremely popular Japanese manga. In the days before social media and online fan communities, there was little connection between TV anime and manga in the United States. That began to change in the 1980s, when feature-length manga-based anime was first shown in American movie theaters.

The early passion for anime in the United States was driven by the twenty-two-hundred-page epic manga *Akira* by Katsuhiro Ōtomo. As journalist Charles C. Mann describes it, "*Akira* is akin to the longest, most grandiose cyberpunk novel ever written, a baroque tale of psychotic teens with telekinetic powers running amok in postapocalyptic Tokyo. . . . Told through Otomo's elegantly detailed black-and-white drawings, *Akira* is arguably the most influential manga ever written."[26]

The manga became even more influential in 1988 after Ōtomo pulled together eight of Japan's largest entertainment and media companies to produce an epic anime based on the story. At the time, the $11 million price tag for the production made *Akira* the costliest big-screen anime to date. The expense paid off when *Akira* became the number one Japanese box office success of 1988. When *Akira* was released in the United States and Europe in 1989, it was a critical and cult hit that was credited with starting the anime boom in the West. Three years after *Akira* appeared in American movie theaters, the first Anime Expo convention was held in San Jose, California. Around 1,750 dedicated fans of Japanese manga and animation were in attendance. Among the guests were Haruhiko Mikimoto, an animator who worked on the *Astro Boy* anime series when it was revived in 1980. Attendance at the Anime Expo continued to grow with the increasing popularity of manga and anime. In 2003 more than 17,500 visited the Anime Expo. In 2022 over 115,000 fans of manga and anime were in attendance. By that time the Japanese anime industry was worth an estimated $27 billion. That number is predicted to grow to $48 billion by 2030 as streaming services such as Netflix and Crunchyroll continue to offer Japanese anime with English subtitles.

## DIZZYING DRAGON SALES

About 60 percent of all anime features created in Japan are based on successful manga, according to anime expert Simon Richmond. When manga sales reach those dizzying levels, they can generate TV series, feature-length anime, and even stage plays and live-action movies for years. Nothing better exemplifies the staying power of a long-running multimedia manga franchise than *Dragon Ball Z*.

The manga series *Dragon Ball*, created by Akira Toriyama, appeared in 520 chapters in *Weekly Shōnen Jump* from 1984 to 1995. The story follows the exploits of Goku, an orphaned alien who grows up on Earth and struggles to become more powerful as

> "*Dragon Ball* [anime] is synonymous with explosive brawls and over-the-top action sequences, with dashes of comedy providing levity in between."[27]
>
> —Tracy Brown, film reviewer

he fights humans, other aliens, androids, and gods. As *Los Angeles Times* reviewer Tracy Brown describes the story, "*Dragon Ball* is synonymous with explosive brawls and over-the-top action sequences, with dashes of comedy providing levity in between."[27]

The *Dragon Ball* manga produced two anime series with over five hundred episodes: *Dragon Ball* and *Dragon Ball Z*, which were broadcast in Japan from 1986 to 1996. Another anime series, *Dragon Ball GT*, was produced in 1997. The American com-

The 1988 anime Akira (pictured) became number one in the Japanese box office. It was released the next year in the United States and Europe and is credited with starting the anime boom in the West.

## COWBOY BEBOP: A MANGA-TO-ANIME CLASSIC

Many popular anime are based on manga series that have hundreds of chapters. But the anime series *Cowboy Bebop* was developed from manga that had only a short run. The eight-chapter space western was published in a Japanese manga magazine for a year in 1997. *Cowboy Bebop* follows a ragtag bounty hunter crew known as the Cowboys who travel the universe aboard the spaceship *Bebop* in the year 2071. In 1998 *Cowboy Bebop* was expanded into a critically acclaimed twenty-six-episode anime TV series in Japan. The popularity of the anime exploded after it appeared on the Cartoon Network in the United States in 2001. The anime continued to air on the network for thirteen years.

The original TV anime of *Cowboy Bebop* was still streaming on Netflix, Crunchyroll, and other services in 2022. The story's long run is held up as an example of a great story that continues to attract new fans for decades. As anime journalist Jonathan Clements explains, "In Japan it was widely understood that *Cowboy Bebop* was lightning in a bottle—that it was a fantastic synergy of creative talent that you couldn't explain."

Quoted in Tyler Aquilina, "The Ballad of *Cowboy Bebop*: How an Oddball Japanese Series Became an Anime Landmark," *Entertainment Weekly*, November 19, 2021. https://ew.com.

---

pany Viz Media began publishing *Dragon Ball Z* manga in English in 1998. The translated Japanese anime series first appeared on the Cartoon Network in 2001, and sales of the *Dragon Ball Z* manga in the United States took off. In the years that followed, fans of Goku could follow his exploits in the anime series *Dragon Ball Z Kai* (2009), *Dragon Ball Super* (2015), and *Super Dragon Ball Heroes* (2018).

Television anime are only part of the *Dragon Ball* story. Since 1986 twenty full-length anime films have been released. The most recent, *Dragon Ball Super: Super Hero* dropped in 2022. The critically acclaimed anime, written by Toriyama, earned over $35 million. And even as fans flock to see the latest full-length anime, interest remains high for the manga that started it all. By 2022 over 303 million tankōbon volumes of the original *Dragon Ball* manga had been sold worldwide. These sales—combined with a myriad of *Dragon Ball* video games, soundtrack albums, books, figurines, clothes, toys, cards, and other related merchandise—have generated around $25 billion over the lifetime of the franchise.

Dragon Ball *merchandise, including figurines like these pictured, contributes to the tens of billions of dollars that the* Dragon Ball *franchise has generated over its lifetime.*

## A FULLMETAL *FRANCHISE*

Popular manga, even those that generate billions of dollars, often rely on the talents of a single creator. And the mangaka at the center of a multimedia whirlwind has little time to rest. Hiromu Arakawa discovered this when she created the runaway hit *Fullmetal Alchemist*. The manga follows the adventures of a twelve-year-old boy named Edward Elric and his younger, armor-plated brother Alphonse. The Elric brothers practice alchemy as they travel through the fictional war-torn land of Amestris. The protagonists are empowered to rearrange the basic building blocks of matter on a molecular level through the use of alchemy.

When *Fullmetal Alchemist* was first published in 2001, it was an instant hit. Before the manga series drew to a close in 2010, Arakawa had created 108 chapters, which sold around 80 million copies. Arakawa is not afraid of hard work; she grew up on a dairy farm in Japan. She milked cows while taking oil painting classes for seven years. When Arakawa dedicated her life to manga in 1998 at age twenty-five, she understood that success required great dedication.

Two years after *Fullmetal Alchemist* debuted in 2001, Arakawa helped develop the anime series. While drawing dozens of manga pages every month, Arakawa worked with producers to write story lines and flesh out characters. She also worked on a second anime adaption, the 2010 *Fullmetal Alchemist: Brotherhood*. This was created as Arakawa was writing the final chapters of the manga. And Arakawa was involved in many other aspects of her *Fullmetal* franchise, as manga journalist Caitlin Donovan writes:

> "Not only did [mangaka Hiromu Arakawa] draw and write 40-plus pages a month, she drew color illustrations, did character designs for *Fullmetal* video games . . . and assisted in production for both anime and movies."[28]
>
> —Caitlin Donovan, manga journalist

Not only did she draw and write 40-plus pages a month, she drew color illustrations, did character designs for *Fullmetal* video games, completed illustrations for light novels, and assisted in production for both anime and movies. In order to coincide with *Brotherhood*'s release, she worked overtime and made the last chapters of *Fullmetal* 60-plus pages a month, with the last chapter over 100 pages long. In addition to all this, she had her first child in 2007 and did not take a maternity leave.[28]

## ONE PIECE *MONEY GENERATOR*

Personal sacrifice goes hand in hand with success for many mangaka whose work is embraced by the public. No one knows this better than Eiichiro Oda, creator of the worldwide manga hit *One Piece*, which has sold a record-breaking 516 million copies since it was first introduced in 1997. Creating the series, which spanned over one thousand chapters by 2022, took a toll on its creator. Oda told interviewers on several occasions that he sleeps only three hours a day, rising at 5:00 a.m. and working until 2:00 a.m., pausing only for meals. Oda maintains his grueling schedule by drinking a lot of coffee and caffeinated cola. And the *One*

## DEMON SLAYER'S REVERSE INFLUX OF FANS

Many manga series are bestsellers before they are turned into anime. But sometimes the release of an anime series helps drive manga sales. This is called *reverse influx*—a reference to large numbers of fans who like an anime so much that they rush to buy the original printed manga.

*Demon Slayer: Kimetsu no Yaiba* by Koyoharu Gotouge is a good example of a manga that benefited from a reverse influx of fans. First published in 2016, *Demon Slayer* sales were about average. That changed in 2019 when the feature-length movie *Demon Slayer: Kimetsu no Yaiba—The Movie: Mugen Train* was released. The anime set a record as the highest-grossing movie opening in Japanese history. And it was so popular the tankōbon volumes of the *Demon Slayer* manga sold 60 million copies globally in the first two weeks after the anime premiered.

Manga sales continued to grow after the first episode of the *Demon Slayer* TV anime premiered in Japan in 2019 and on Nickelodeon's Adult Swim in the United States the following year. The reverse influx caused by the TV anime helped push *Demon Slayer* manga sales even higher. By 2022 the series had sold 150 million copies, making *Demon Slayer* the ninth-best-selling manga of all time.

*Piece* mangaka does not live with his wife and two daughters. He has his own home, where he schedules family visits once a week. Some might say the sacrifice has paid off. *One Piece* is among the most successful multimedia money generators of all time, and Oda's net worth in 2022 was over $200 million.

Most manga and anime fans know that *One Piece* revolves around treasure-hunting young pirate Monkey D. Luffy and his gang, the Straw Hat Pirates. Luffy, wearing his signature straw hat, red vest, and sandals, sets sail to find a mythical treasure called One Piece that would allow him to become King of the Pirates. Luffy is just one of many pirates searching for One Piece, but he has an advantage. After eating a supernatural food called Devil Fruit, his body has developed the properties of rubber. This makes it possible for him to stretch his limbs and body into all sorts of configurations to deliver kicks, punches, headbutts, and other defensive maneuvers.

The *One Piece* anime television series premiered in Japan in 1999 and has been in production ever since. By 2022 over one thousand episodes of the series had been produced. The show has consistently rated among the top animated shows in Japan, and *One Piece* is also an international hit. The story also generated an incredible fourteen feature films from 2000 to 2019. Together these anime productions have made over $511 million as of 2022.

*One Piece* is also a musical hit, responsible for more than one hundred soundtracks from films and the TV series. There are at least fifty-six video games based on the manga, along with ten novels and nine related art books. When taken with the array of toys, clothing, and other *One Piece* items, Oda's pirate story has generated more than $5.5 billion. After completing the one thousandth chapter of *One Piece* in 2021, Oda released a letter to thank his fans: "Words pretty much fail to describe the whirlwind these past 23 years have been. Literally half of my life has revolved around the almighty WEEKLY SERIALIZATION. . . . Your belief in Luffy has led me to believe in all of you, and that is what allows me to continue drawing exactly the kind of manga I want to draw."[29]

## QUIRKY SUPERHEROES

Monkey D. Luffy is one of many manga characters that rely on superhuman powers to deal with any situation, but not all of them possess such extraordinary abilities. One of the most popular anime on Crunchyroll in 2022 was *My Hero Academia*, based on a manga series written and illustrated by Kōhei Horikoshi. The story focuses on Izuku "Deku" Midoriya, who lives in a world where 80 percent of the population, including his parents, were born with some sort of superpower, or Quirk. Each individual's Quirk is unique. Depending on how they use their powers, they are classified as either Heroes or Villains. Like many leading manga characters, Deku is a nerdy teenaged misfit. He was born "Quirkless," meaning without a Quirk. But Deku dreams of achieving the revered celebrity status called Pro Hero. Deku meets with the world's greatest superhero, All Might, who grants him superpowers. This leads Deku to enroll in the prestigious U.A. High School to master his newfound powers.

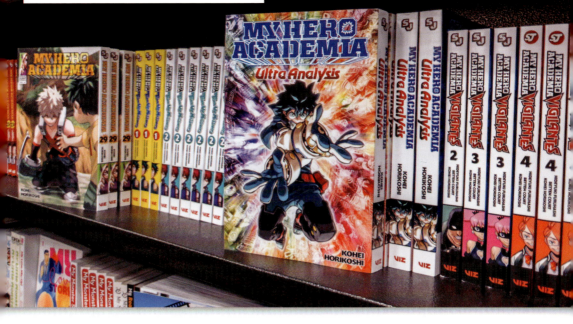

Not all manga characters have extraordinary abilities. This picture shows a volume from *My Hero Academia*, a popular manga series about a world where 80 percent of the population is born with some sort of superpower, or Quirk.

Horikoshi launched *My Hero Academia* in 2014. The manga sold more than seventy-five thousand copies the first week. By the time the series drew to a close in 2022, Horikoshi had produced 306 chapters, combined into 35 tankōbon volumes that sold over 65 million copies total. The manga also produced three major spin-off manga series created by others: *My Hero Academia: Smash!!*, *My Hero Academia: Vigilantes*, and *My Hero Academia: Team-Up Missions*. When it was announced that the series would be animated, the news caught Horikoshi off guard: "I was really surprised. I remember it was decided when the serialization wasn't even a year old, so I felt kind of lost all of the sudden. Then I hurriedly started telling my friends and family the news . . . and they were all happy for me, which is the moment that I finally had the realization that went something like 'ah, this is great, I'm getting an anime.'"[30]

> "I finally had the realization that went something like 'ah, this is great, I'm getting an anime.'"[30]
>
> —Kōhei Horikoshi, creator of *My Hero Academia*

46

The first season of the anime *My Hero Academia* premiered in the United States and Japan in 2016. By the time the sixth season was released in 2022, the anime was attracting millions of views on Crunchyroll. Like many other popular manga, *My Hero Academia* quickly became a multimedia monster. Three feature-length anime films were produced during 2017 to 2020: *My Hero Academia: Two Heroes*, *My Hero Academia: Heroes Rising*, and *My Hero Academia: World Heroes' Mission*. The story was used as the basis for video games, three stage plays, and a dizzying array of merchandise, including action figures, backpacks, T-shirts, card games, and Blu-ray DVD sets.

*My Hero Academia* is one of more than one thousand anime shows offered on Crunchyroll, which delivers content to over 100 million users worldwide. Anime lovers can also find some of their favorite manga-based shows like *Demon Slayer*, *Cowboy Bebop*, and *Neon Genesis Evangelion* on Netflix, Amazon Prime, and Hulu. These and other streaming services have created a new wave of anime accessibility that has allowed fans to enjoy older shows and discover new ones. This anime enthusiasm would not be possible without the hard work, dedication, and creativity of the manga artists who originated the creative concepts and characters behind the cartoons. These artists have inspired legions of dedicated fans who keep manga and anime alive.

# CHAPTER FIVE

# COSPLAY CULTURE

Every year around 150,000 people attend San Diego Comic-Con, the world's largest comic book convention. Around one in ten guests arrive wearing costumes of their favorite comic book characters. Among the estimated 15,000 costumed attendees, Wonder Woman, the Joker, and Spider-Man are always in abundance. The halls of Comic-Con also include a profusion of manga characters ranging from Sailor Moon to *Dragon Ball*'s Master Roshi.

Dressing up like a comic book character is called cosplay, a mashup of the words *costume* and *role-play*. The term was coined in 1984 when Japanese studio head Nobuyuki Takahashi attended the World Science Fiction Convention in Los Angeles. Takahashi was amazed when he saw hundreds of people wearing costumes of their favorite characters from Japanese science-fiction manga. Since that time, cosplay has become a favorite activity of dedicated fans of manga and anime, especially at comic conventions. Many spend days—or weeks—creating their costumes and trying out different makeup and hairstyles. At the convention, they put in extra time to make sure nothing is amiss. Journalist Jessica Roar writes:

> Each day, cosplayers wake up super early to make sure their costume and makeup are perfect. . . . Cosplayers have to leave the [convention] area several

times throughout the day to touch up their makeup or fix their wig. . . . [And] all the people at the con make the environment hot. Can you imagine walking around in a full body suit with multiple layers? Cosplayers have to do extra work to stay hydrated and cool during events.[31]

## FANATICAL FANS

Many people who regularly engage in cosplay are part of *otaku* culture. *Otaku* is a Japanese word that describes someone who has an obsessive interest in manga and anime. English terms that correspond to *otaku* are *geek* or *nerd*, but these words often have negative connotations. *Otaku*, on the other hand, has lost its negative meaning in Japan, where it has become a prominent and accepted aspect of pop culture.

> "Each day, cosplayers wake up super early to make sure their costume and makeup are perfect."[31]
>
> —Jessica Roar, journalist

The center of otaku culture in Tokyo is the Akihabara neighborhood. Known as the "geek district," the streets are lined with manga-themed bars and cafés. Dozens of multistory manga stores with pulsating lights blast loud music. Young, mostly female employees dressed as manga characters and holding megaphones stand in front of the stores, urging passersby to stop in and shop. Inside, shoppers can find manga, DVDs, games, and all types of manga-related merchandise, including chocolates, bottled water, clothing, playing cards, headphones, and plastic dolls.

Stores like Animate Akihabara, which sells hundreds of manga costumes, is an otaku paradise. But the most creative and dedicated cosplayers prefer to make their own costumes. Some spend hundreds of dollars just for fabric and buttons. They spend much more to buy wigs, shoes, jewelry, and other accessories.

The Akihabara neighborhood, pictured here, is the center of otaku culture in Tokyo. Its streets are lined with manga-themed bars and cafés.

## THE COSPLAY SUMMIT

One goal of such detailed, time-consuming, and costly preparations is personal satisfaction. Another goal for many otaku is to put their creativity on display. This happens at any number of public gatherings. One of the gatherings to which otaku flock is the World Cosplay Summit, or WCS, held every August in Nagoya, Japan.

The WCS was founded in 2002 to promote Japanese culture to an international audience through manga, anime, and cosplay. The first summit featured cosplayers from three countries outside Japan—Germany, Italy, and France. On its tenth anniversary the WCS hosted cosplayers from twenty-four countries, including Australia, Finland, Malaysia, and the United Kingdom. By 2022 cosplayers from forty countries on nearly every continent could be found at the WCS. Many participated in the Cosplay Championship costume contest. Winners were from Canada, Chile, China, India, Indonesia, Mexico, Spain, and Thailand.

The Osu Cosplay Parade is one of the highlights of the WCS. Hundreds of people dressed as manga characters stroll down the main street of the downtown Nagoya shopping district, carrying signs that identify their native countries. As manga expert Anna Toccoli writes, "On event days, it's not rare to see characters from your favorite [manga or anime] taking the subway or having lunch at a family restaurant."[32]

> "It's not rare to see characters from your favorite [manga or anime] taking the subway or having lunch at a family restaurant."[32]
>
> —Anna Toccoli, manga expert

In 2022 an unnamed French cosplayer dressed like Monkey D. Luffy said, "Cosplay is a peaceful hobby because people from all over the world can enjoy it together."[33] To keep things peaceful, WCS promoters have fairly strict rules for participants. Costumes cannot be too skimpy, and while many manga feature futuristic weapons, dangerous objects are banned from the event.

Otaku in North America do not have to travel to Japan to enjoy mingling in cosplayer communities. Every February, during Presidents' Day weekend, fans of manga, anime, and video games gather in National Harbor, Maryland, to celebrate Katsucon. The

## LIGHTING UP A CITY

The dedication of otaku fans can be seen in Fukuoka, Japan, where the tallest building, called the Fukuoka Tower, stands 768 feet (234 m) above the city. The corporation that maintains the building allows the public to pay to light up the building in their choice of colors to mark special occasions. The cost to light the tower for ten minutes in red, blue, green, orange, purple, or pink is around $300.

When the Fukuoka Tower Corporation first introduced the idea in 2020, it was expected that people would pay to light the building for anniversaries. But dozens of requests came from manga lovers. One fan paid to turn the tower purple to celebrate Tokiya's birthday; Tokiya is a character from the manga and anime franchise *Uta no Prince-sama*, and purple is his favorite color. When the lighting event was live streamed on social media, tens of thousands of Tokiya lovers tuned in to watch. Another dedicated fan paid to celebrate the birthday of Noriaki Kakyoin from the manga *JoJo's Bizarre Adventure*. The Fukuoka Tower was lit up green to represent the ghostly power called Hierophant Green that can be summoned by Noriaki.

Competitors from the Netherlands perform at the World Cosplay Summit in 2019. The summit is held annually in Nagoya, Japan, and is very popular among otaku.

festival was first conceived in 1995 by Katsucon Entertainment Inc. (KEI) as a way to educate people about Japanese pop culture. In 2022 around twenty-three thousand people attended the annual three-day festival. There were craft workshops, costume contests, and plenty of meetups for cosplayers to interact and share ideas. As KEI treasurer Christian Savage explains, "The atmosphere is a supportive one. A lot of attendees like to share their creativity, and the meetups spur ideas from those in the community to work together on group projects."[34]

# TIKTOK COSPLAY

Sharing ideas and interests became more difficult with the COVID-19 pandemic that began in 2020. Most conventions—including Katsu-con, Comic-Con, and other major meetups—were canceled. During that period many cosplayers began to show off their costumes on TikTok. While Instagram and Facebook have long been popular sites for cosplay displays, TikTok's focus on dancing and singing added a new dimension to cosplay. According to Japanese pop culture expert Sydney Reynolds, "In the videos they make, TikTok cosplayers can lip-sync to songs in character, act out their character's reactions to new situations, or recreate a character's iconic catchphrase. TikTok is a whole new space for creative innovation, and some cosplayers decided to take full advantage of the platform."[35]

Some manga-inspired cosplayers have attracted a huge number of views and likes on TikTok. In 2022 a cosplayer named Bestiny found a clever way to portray the lovable four-year-old telepath Anya from the popular action/comedy manga and anime series *Spy x Family*. The video went viral, racking up over 3.3 million views and more than three hundred thousand loves.

> "TikTok cosplayers can lip-sync to songs in character, act out their character's reactions to new situations, or recreate a character's iconic catchphrase."[35]
>
> —Sydney Reynolds, Japanese pop culture expert

The manga for *Spy x Family*, written and illustrated by Tatsuya Endo, was first serialized on the Shōnen Jump app in 2019. The English digital publication became one of the best-selling manga in recent years, leading to an anime adaptation that premiered in 2022. The story's central character, Anya, is adopted by parents who have very unusual top secret jobs. Her father, Loid, is a world-class spy, and her mother, Yor, is an assassin. Much of the humor is delivered by Anya, who quickly became an otaku favorite because of the emotions she exhibits.

Bestiny captured the essence of the character by creating a rotating cardboard head with four of Anya's iconic expressions. While

## OTAKU FASHIONS

Conservatively tailored suits are the top fashion choice in Tokyo's business and government circles. In other parts of Tokyo, otaku-influenced dress adds color and flare to the city. One of the most popular otaku styles in Japan is called the Lolita look. This fashion style consists of frilly dresses, parasols, and bows that give the wearer a very youthful, doll-like appearance. Some carry around stuffed animals to look as young as possible. Others give the Lolita look a twist by adding dark, goth-style makeup or even using makeup and accessories to take on the appearance of a Lolita zombie or witch.

Another popular otaku fashion is named for the Harajuku neighborhood in Tokyo where it originated. Harajuku fashionistas celebrate what is called a weird girl aesthetic. They create crazy-looking mismatched outfits that mix bright colors, plaid, tie-dye, fake fur, platform shoes, and elaborate wigs. An androgynous style known as visual kei has roots in American heavy metal and punk rock and is often worn by musicians. Men and women who dress in visual kei fashions wear heavy makeup, flamboyant costumes, and elaborate hairstyles.

Anya's pink floppy hair stays in place above it, Bestiny spins a four-sided box painted with different expressions on each side. One side shows Anya's crying face, another her famous dumbstruck expression. At the end of the eleven-second video, Bestiny's Anya strikes a superhero pose with her hands on her hips and her hair blowing in the wind. Many of the thousands of comments on the video praised Bestiny's work, saying it is creative, unique, and the best cosplay video of Anya ever made. Bestiny was among the first to portray Anya on TikTok, but certainly not the last. The TikTok Anya Cosplay link displays multiple videos with a shared total of nearly 8 million views.

## DRESS-UP DARLINGS

When cosplayers don the clothes, wigs, and makeup of their favorite characters, it might be said that life is imitating art. But art can also imitate life in the world of manga when stories focus on characters who love cosplay. That idea drives the plot of *My Dress-Up Darling*. The romantic comedy manga with a heavy emphasis on cosplay has seen sales increase since the anime was released in 2022.

*My Dress-Up Darling* was written and illustrated by Shinichi Fukuda, who studied the art of cosplaying when she was writing the manga series. The story has two main characters. Wakana Gojo is an introverted high school student who secretly crafts *hina* dolls, beautiful Japanese ornamental dolls that portray the emperor, empress, and others in the royal court. (Hina dolls have been used in religious celebrations for more than a thousand years.) Wakana is traumatized after being mocked by schoolmates as a boy who plays with dolls. But a beautiful, popular girl named Marin Kitagawa notices Wakana's talents when she sees him bent over a sewing machine making a doll's costume. Marin convinces Wakana to help her make the best cosplay outfit ever.

*My Dress-Up Darling* is notable for its realistic depiction of cosplayers, as essayist Daryl Harding writes:

> Everything from the stores Gojo and Marin use to buy their gear to the locations where they take cosplay photos are perfectly recreated from the standpoint of real cosplayers living in the real world. At times, the show could almost be a tutorial on how to cosplay in Japan. . . . By showing off all the different aspects, cosplay making, location scouting, photography, and the cost behind it all, *My Dress-Up Darling* is informing the layman on just how much goes into the hobby and how expensive it is.[36]

Harding calls *My Dress-Up Darling* a love letter to the cosplay community, which uses the power of the internet and translation to introduce the hobby to people throughout the world. However, as a Japanese cosplayer named Yamohachiko tweeted, there is one aspect of *My Dress-Up Darling* that is not realistic. The anime shows Wakana making a costume for another person. "In most cases," Yamohachiko says, "the cosplayer prepares their own costumes and makeup. But perhaps [Wakana] exists because Marin is very cute."[37]

## A CULTURE OF CUTE

The term *cute* has special meaning in Japan, where the word *kawaii* translates as "cuteness." The word, which is frequently used in Japan, is sometimes pronounced kawaiiiiiiiiiiiiiii to indicate extreme cuteness. The character Hello Kitty is a Japanese kawaiiiiiiiiiiiiii superstar. The cute white cat with no mouth can be found in a range of products, from manga and anime to a Hello Kitty–themed bullet train in Japan. With the strong focus on kawaii, it is no surprise that characters like Hello Kitty are most

*The cute white Hello Kitty character is a Japanese kawaii superstar. Kawaii characters like Hello Kitty are often imitated by cosplayers, as pictured here.*

imitated by cosplayers. Many manga and anime characters are similar to the kawaii cat, who has a big head on a small body, huge round eyes, and a tiny nose that make her seem cute, vulnerable, and alluring.

Some might wonder how millions of people can spend their lives dressing up as cartoon characters. But many cosplayers consider their activities a type of performance art. This allows them to show off their artistic spirits in a culture that traditionally emphasizes the needs of society over individual desires. While highlighting their individuality, cosplayers are also part of a worldwide community that values otaku culture.

With interest in manga and anime skyrocketing, the number of otaku is expected to grow with it. As artist and blogger David Fox writes, "This unique subculture has brought joy and entertainment to millions of fans around the world, and shows no signs of slowing down anytime soon!"[38]

> "[Otaku] subculture has brought joy and entertainment to millions of fans around the world, and shows no signs of slowing down anytime soon!"[38]
>
> —David Fox, artist and blogger

# SOURCE NOTES

## INTRODUCTION: THE WORLD LOVES MANGA

1. Quoted in Deb Aoki, "Streaming Anime Lifts Manga Sales," PW, May 7, 2021. www.publishersweekly.com.
2. Quoted in Deb Aoki, "Manga Sales Up, Exhibitors Down at San Diego Comic-Con," PW, July 28, 2022. www.publishersweekly.com.
3. Quoted in Misaki C. Kido, "Interview: Eiichiro Oda," Viz, April 2, 2012. www.viz.com.
4. Quoted in Goodreads, "Osamu Tezuka: Quotes," 2021. www.goodreads.com.

## CHAPTER ONE: THE EVOLUTION OF MANGA

5. Doug McGray, "Japan's Gross National Cool," *Foreign Policy*, November 11, 2009. https://foreignpolicy.com.
6. Frederik L. Schodt, *Dreamland Japan*. Berkeley, CA: Stone Bridge, 2011, pp. 21–22.
7. Sheri Le and Will Dodds, "Manga: Evolution," Right Stuf, 2021. www.rightstufanime.com.
8. Quoted in John Canemaker, "The Kid from *Hogan's Alley*," *New York Times*, December 17, 1995. www.nytimes.com.
9. Quoted in Van Gogh Alive, "Artists in 60 Seconds: Tezuka Osamu," 2021. www.vangoghgenova.it.
10. Frederik L. Schodt, *The Astro Boy Essays*. Berkeley, CA: Stone Bridge, 2007, p. 30.

## CHAPTER TWO: MANGA FOR EVERYONE

11. Jessica Roar, *Otaku 101*. Los Angeles: HowExpert, 2018, p. 8.
12. Paul Gravett, *Manga: Sixty Years of Japanese Comics*. New York: Harper Design International, 2004, p. 59.
13. Quoted in Mark W. MacWilliams, ed., *Japanese Visual Culture*. Armonk, NY: East Gate, 2008, pp. 123–24.
14. Quoted in Toni Johnson-Woods, ed., *Manga: An Anthology of Global and Cultural Perspectives*. New York: Continuum, 2010, p. 95.

## CHAPTER THREE: REINVENTING MANGA

15. Kadi Yao Tay, "African Webtoons Worth Checking Out on Webtoon and Tapas," Squid Magazine, 2021. https://squidmag.ink.

16. Tae Yim, "What Is the Difference Between a Webtoon and a Manga?," Quora, 2020. www.quora.com.

17. Quoted in Bookworm, "Lore Olympus," 2022. https://bookworm bernardsville.indielite.org.

18. Quoted in Rob Salkowitz, "Webtoon Is Paying Its Creators Millions to Make Mobile Comics," *Forbes*, July 18, 2022. www.forbes.com.

19. Quoted in Brahidaliz Martinez, "A Magical Destiny of His Own: An Interview with Vincent Kao (the Kao), Creator of 'Magical Boy,'" The Geekiary, July 8, 2021. https://thegeekiary.com.

20. Quoted in George Gene Gustines and Matt Stevens, "Comics That Read Top to Bottom Are Bringing in New Readers," *New York Times*, July 23, 2022. www.nytimes.com.

21. Quoted in Azario Lopez, "Webcomic 'The Beginning After the End' to Receive Print Release," Noisy Pixel, October 8, 2021. https://noisypixel.net.

22. Quoted in Julija Neje, "This Artist Shares What It's Like to Grow Up in an Indian Family, Quickly Gets over 1 Million Views on Webtoon," Bored Panda, 2018. www.boredpanda.com.

23. Quoted in Dhruvi Joshi, "Kross Comics and Kross Pictures' to Grow in India and Produce a Lot More K-Webtoons Based K-Dramas: Co-Founder Hyunwoo Thomas Kim," Animation Xpress, June 7, 2022. www.animationxpress.com.

24. Lisa Fernandes, "Review: I Am Totally Weak for Wayne Family Adventures," WWAC, September 5, 2022. https://womenwriteabout comics.com.

25. Yim, "What Is the Difference Between a Webtoon and a Manga?"

## CHAPTER FOUR: FROM MANGA TO ANIME

26. Charles C. Mann, "The Giants of Anime Are Coming," *Wired*, September 2004. www.wired.com.

27. Tracy Brown, "Review: The New 'Dragon Ball' Movie Shines a Deserving Spotlight on the Franchise's Best Dad," *Los Angeles Times*, August 18, 2022. www.latimes.com.

28. Caitlin Donovan, "Get to Know a Manga Artist: The Unstoppable Hiromu Arakawa," Mary Sue, October 14, 2014. www.themarysue .com.

29. Quoted in Joseph Luster, "*One Piece* 1000th Chapter Celebration Has the Series Going All Out," *Otaku USA Magazine*, January 3, 2021. https://otakuusamagazine.com.
30. Quoted in Nakurawari, "The Real Horikoshi Pre-Anime Interview," Reddit, 2016. www.reddit.com.

## CHAPTER FIVE: COSPLAY CULTURE

31. Jessica Roar, *Otaku 101*. Los Angeles: HowExpert, p. 24.
32. Anna Toccoli, "Anime, Manga, and Video Games: The Otaku Events You Shouldn't Miss in Japan," Voyapon, September 14, 2022. https://voyapon.com.
33. Quoted in Sankei Shimbun, "Cosplayers from All Over the World Gather for Nagoya Parade," Japan Forward, August 26, 2022. https://japan-forward.com.
34. Quoted in Nicole Savas, "Katsucon: Where Cosplayers and Japanese Culture Collide," Pop Insider, January 20, 2020. https://the popinsider.com.
35. Sydney Reynolds, "How TikTok Created a Community When Cosplayers Lost Conventions," Pop Insider, August 30, 2021. https://thepopinsider.com.
36. Daryl Harding, "How *My Dress-Up Darling* Taps Into Cosplay Culture by Being Grounded in Reality," Crunchyroll, April 15, 2022. www.crunchyroll.com.
37. Quoted in Harding, "How *My Dress-Up Darling* Taps Into Cosplay Culture by Being Grounded in Reality."
38. David Fox, "Otaku Subculture History," DavidCharlesFox.com, 2022. https://davidcharlesfox.com.

# FOR FURTHER RESEARCH

## BOOKS

Robert M. Henderson, *A Quick Guide to Anime and Manga*. San Diego: ReferencePoint, 2022.

Stuart A. Kallen, *The Art and Artists of Manga*. San Diego: ReferencePoint, 2022.

Jessica Roar, *Otaku 101*. Los Angeles: HowExpert, 2018.

Gianni Simone, *Otaku Japan: The Fascinating World of Japanese Manga, Anime, Gaming, Cosplay, Toys, Idols and More!* North Clarendon, VT: Tuttle, 2021.

Akira Toriyama, Dragon Ball*: A Visual History*. San Francisco: VIZ Media, 2019.

## INTERNET SOURCES

Brigid Alverson, "20 Years Ago, *Dragon Ball Z* Came to America to Stay," CBR, September 18, 2016. www.cbr.com.

Deb Aoki, "Streaming Anime Lifts Manga Sales," PW, May 7, 2021. www.publishersweekly.com.

Brahidaliz Martinez, "A Magical Destiny of His Own: An Interview with Vincent Kao (the Kao), Creator of 'Magical Boy,'" Geekiary, July 8, 2021. https://thegeekiary.com.

Tara McGowan, "Welcome to the 'Land of Children' (*Kodomo no kuni*): Courtesy of a Gift from the Friends of Princeton University Library," Princeton University Library, February 1, 2019. https://blogs.princeton.edu.

Kadi Yao Tay, "African Webtoons Worth Checking Out on Webtoon and Tapas," Squid Magazine, 2021. https://squidmag.ink.

# WEBSITES

### Anime News Network

www.animenewsnetwork.com
This is one of the most popular online news sources for anime and manga. In addition to news, it provides reviews, press releases, and anime convention reports.

### Manga Plus

https://mangaplus.shueisha.co.jp
The publisher of *Weekly Shōnen Jump* and other magazines hosts this website, which offers sample pages from the latest manga, news events, artist and editor interviews, and free wallpapers and icons.

### *One Piece*

https://one-piece.com
The English-language version of the *One Piece* website features details about the more than one thousand chapter manga drawn by Eiichiro Oda. Readers can learn about the story and the characters, watch anime clips, and shop for related merchandise.

### Tezuka Osamu

https://tezukaosamu.net/en
The official website of Osamu Tezuka features drawings and descriptions about more than two hundred manga and anime series, along with character biographies and other information.

### Tokyo Otaku Mode

https://otakumode.com
*Otaku* describes a young Japanese person obsessed with manga and anime. This site covers the latest pop culture news from Japan, with a focus on manga, anime, games, music, and fashion.

### Webtoon

www.webtoons.com
This popular South Korean website publishes thousands of digital comics formatted for smartphones and created by independent artists and storytellers throughout the world.

# INDEX

*Note: Boldface page numbers indicate illustrations.*

Aira Misono (character), 27
akahon (red books), 12
Akihabara neighborhood (Tokyo), 49, **50**
*Akira* (anime/manga), 38–39, **40**
*Akira* (manga), 38–39
anime (animated cartoons), 4
   adaptation of manga into, 17
   first, 14
   first US convention for, 39
   manga intertwined with, 38
   reverse influx with manga, 44
   on streaming services, 47
Anime News Network (website), 62
Arakawa, Hiromu, 42–43
Aso, Yutaka, 11
*Astro Boy* (TV anime series), **12**, 14

*Batman: Wayne Family Adventures*
   (webtoon), 36–37
*The Beginning After the End* (*TBATE*,
   webtoon), 33
*Best Friend* (magazine), 24
Blackbeard, Bill, 10
Black Panther, 36, **36**
Bouquillard, Jocelyn, 11
*Bringing Up Father* (comic), 11
Brown, Tracy, 40
*Brown Paperbag* (Indian webtoon), 34

*Case Closed* (shonen manga), 22
Chavez, Ed, 5
Clements, Jonathan, 41
Comic-Con (comic book convention, San
   Diego), 48
cosplay, 48–49
   competitors in, **52**
   public gatherings for, 50–52
   on TikTok, 53–54
*Cowboy Bebop* (anime series), 41
Crunchyroll (streaming service), 41, 45, 47

*Demon Slayer: Kimetsu no Yaiba* (anime/
   manga series), 44
Dodds, Will, 10
Donovan, Caitlin, 43

*Doraemon* (kodomo manga), 20–21
*Doraemon: Nobita's New Dinosaur*
   (feature-length anime), 21
*Dragon Ball* (manga series), 39
   anime series inspired by, 40–41
   merchandise from, **42**

*Easygoing Daddy* (comic), 11
Eisner Comic Industry Award, 30–31
Endo, Tatsuya, 53

Fernandes, Lisa, 37
Fox, David, 57
Fujiazuki, 27
Fukuda, Shinichi, 55
Fukuoka Tower (Japan), 51
*Fullmetal Alchemist* (manga series), 42
   anime inspired by, 43
Fuyuki23 (webtoon creator), 33

Gotouge, Koyoharu, 44
Gravett, Paul, 22, 24

Hagio, Moto, 25
Harding, Daryl, 55
Hello Kitty (character), **56**, 56–57
Hicks, Faith Erin, 30
Hogan's Alley (comic), 10
Hokusai, Katsushika, 9, **9**, 11
Horibuchi, Seiji, 15

isekai stories, 33

Jae-won, Lee, 35

Kao, Vincent, 31, 32–33
Katsucon festival (MD), 51–52
kawaii (cuteness), 56
K-drama (South Korean television soap
   operas), 35
Kim, Hyunwoo Thomas, 35
Kim, Ken, 31
Kitazawa, Rakuten, 11
Koda, Momoko, 27
kodomo manga (manga for children),
   18–21
   roots of, 20
Kodomo no kuni ("Land of Children"), 19, 20

Kross Komics, 34–35

Le, Sheri, 10
LGBTQ+ story lines, 26–27, 33
LINE Webtoon (India), 33–34
*Lone Wolf and Cub* (manga), 15–16
Lord, Jessica, 15
*Lore Olympus* (webtoon), 29–30

*Magical Boy* (manga), 31–33
Magnificent 24s (female manga artists), 24–25, 26
manga
    for boys, 21–22
    for children, 18–21
    digital, 28–29
    format of, **6**, 6–7
    for girls, 23–26
    influence of Western comics on, 10–11
    number published annually, 18
    origin of term, 11
    subgenres of, 26–27
Manga Plus (website), 62
manhwa (South Korean manga), 28, 29, **30**
Mann, Charles C., 38
McGowan, Tara M., 20
McGray, Doug, 8
McManus, George, 11
*Mighty Atom* (manga series), **12**, 14, 38
    *See also Astro Boy*
Mikimoto, Haruhiko, 39
Monkey D. Luffy (character), 45
*My Dress-Up Darling* (anime/manga), 54–55
*My Hero Academia* (manga/anime series), 45–47, **46**

Naruto (anime/manga series), 22, 23
Naruto Uzumaki (character), **23**
*New Treasure Island* (comic), 13
*No Longer Heroine* (manga series), 27

Oda, Eiichiro, 5–6, 7, 43–44
*One Piece* (manga/anime series), 43–44
One Piece (website), 62
Oshima, Yumiko, 25
otaku (anime/manga fan), 49
otaku fashion, 54
Ōtomo, Katsuhiro, 38
Outcault, R.F., 10

*Pokémon Adventures* (kodomo manga), 18, **19**
Prough, Jennifer, 26–27

reverse influx, 44

Reynolds, Sydney, 53
Roar, Jessica, 22, 48–49

*Sailor Moon* (manga series), 15, 31
    main characters in, **16**
*Sailor Moon* (manga, anime series), 16–17
*The Saint's Magic Power Is Omnipotent* (manga series), 27
Savage, Christian, 52
Schodt, Frederik L., 8, 14
Sentar, Lianne, 4
sexuality, manga subgenres exploring, 26–27
Shinichi Kudō (character), 21
*Shōjo Comic* (magazine), 24
shojo manga (manga for girls), 23–26
    female warrior in, **25**
Shōnen Club (manga), 21, 24–25
shonen manga (manga for boys), 21–22
Smyth, Rachel, 29–31
Son, Michael, 33
*Spy x Family* (anime/magna series), 53

Tachibana, Yuka, 27
Takahash, Nobuyuki, 48
Takahashi, Mizuki, 26
Takeuchi, Naoko, 15
Tapas (digital publishing platform), 31
Tapastry (digital publishing platform), 32
Tay, Kadi Yao, 29
Tezuka, Osamu, 6, 7, 12–15, 38
    website of, 62
Toccoli, Anna, 51
Tokyo Otaku Mode (website), 62
*Tokyo Puck* (magazine), 11
Toriyama, Akira, 39, 41
TurtleMe (webtoon creator), 33

ukiyo-e (floating world pictures), 9–10

*The Wave* (print), **9**
webcomics, 28
Webtoon (app), 28–29, **30**, 62
webtoons
    American, 35–37
    Indian, 33–34
    South Korean, 29–33
woodblock printing, 9
World Cosplay Summit (Nagoya, Japan), 50–51, **52**
World War II, 12

Yellow Kid, 10–11
Yim, Tae, 29, 37